Sandy Creek
NEW YORK

An Imprint of Sterling Publishing
1166 Avenue of The Americas
New York, NY, 10036

Words in **bold** are explained in the glossary on page 60.

Text © 2014 by QEB Publishing, Inc.
Illustrations © 2014 by QEB Publishing, Inc.

This 2014 edition published by Sandy Creek.

ISBN 978-1-4351-5530-5

Manufactured in Guangdong, China
Lot #:
4 6 8 10 9 7 5 3
11/15

Contents

Solar System

The Solar System is made up of the Sun and all the objects that circle, or **orbit**, around it. These include the planets and their moons.

Sun

Venus

Mars

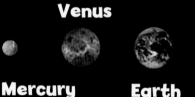

Mercury

Earth

« The Sun is a bright star at the center of the Solar System.

Jupiter

There are eight planets in the Solar System, including Earth. Thousands of rocks, or asteroids, and millions of icy chunks, known as comets, also travel around the Sun.

Saturn

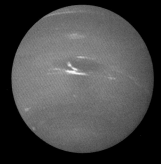

Uranus

Neptune

The Sun

The Sun is a ball of hot, bright, burning gas. It is the nearest star to Earth.

>> The Sun is so big that a million Earths could fit inside it.

Sun

⌃ The planets circle, or orbit, the Sun.

You should never look straight at the Sun. It is so bright that it can damage your eyes.

⋁ **The Sun provides Earth with light and warmth.**

Mercury

Mercury is the planet nearest to the Sun. It is the smallest planet in the Solar System.

Earth

Mercury

The Moon

⌃ Mercury is only a little bigger than Earth's Moon.

≫ Mercury is covered with craters. These were made by meteorites and asteroids hitting the planet.

Like Earth, Mercury has a hard surface, but it has no **atmosphere**. No wind ever blows there, and clouds never drift across its skies.

⋁ **This crater on Mercury looks as if it has a smiley face!**

Venus

Venus is the second planet from the Sun. It is the hottest planet in the Solar System.

˅ Venus is about the same size as Earth.

Venus

Sun

Venus

˄ Venus can often be seen as a bright point of light after sunset or before sunrise.

Venus

Earth

Venus is surrounded by thick clouds of poisonous gases. Beneath these, the rocky planet is covered with high mountains and deep valleys.

▼ This is what Venus looks like beneath its thick atmosphere.

Earth

Earth is the third planet from the Sun. It is the only planet where we know life exists.

>> **Earth is hot on the inside but cool on the surface.**

Earth is a rocky planet covered by dry land, deep oceans, and frozen **ice caps**. It is surrounded by a layer of air, called the atmosphere.

Earth's hot core

>> Earth spins around once every 24 hours. The side facing the Sun has daytime. The other side has nighttime.

Sun

Daytime

Nighttime

<< Earth's atmosphere wraps around the planet like a thin blanket.

The Moon

The Moon is a rocky ball about a quarter of the Earth's size. It circles the Earth once every 28 days.

⌄ **There is no weather on the Moon. It is never cloudy or wet there.**

Earth

The Moon

>> This phase is called a crescent moon.

We can only see the part of the Moon that reflects the Sun's light. As the Moon circles Earth, it looks like it is changing shape. The shapes are called phases.

⌃ Parts of the Moon are covered with dark "seas" where lava once flowed.

Mars

Mars is a rocky, red planet about half the size of Earth. It is the fourth planet from the Sun.

⌄ Mars has lots of volcanoes. One of them, Olympus Mons, is the biggest volcano in the Solar System.

∨ Mars is red because of rusty iron in its soil.

∧ Several robots, known as Mars rovers, have been sent to explore Mars.

Long ago, Mars was warm and wet, and had lakes and rivers. There may once have been life there. Today, the only water on Mars is frozen in its ice caps or is frozen deep underground.

Jupiter

Jupiter is the fifth planet from the Sun and the biggest planet in the Solar System.

Io

Europa

Ganymede

Callisto

≪ Jupiter has more than 63 moons. The biggest moons are labeled here.

>> The Great Red Spot is a huge storm in Jupiter's atmosphere.

 << You could fit 1,321 Earths inside Jupiter!

Jupiter is a **gas giant** with no solid surface. Its swirling bands of cloud and many storms make it a very colorful planet.

Saturn

Saturn is the sixth planet from the Sun. It is surrounded by wide rings, and has more than 60 moons. Its biggest moon is called Titan.

⌃ Saturn is the second-largest planet in the Solar System.

<< **Titan is covered with lakes, rivers, and seas. These are made of liquid methane, not water.**

Saturn is a gas giant with a small, rocky core. This huge planet takes 30 years to travel around the Sun.

>> **Saturn's rings are made from millions of lumps of ice.**

Uranus

˅ Uranus has a set
of very faint rings.

Uranus is the seventh
planet from the Sun.
It takes Uranus
84 years to travel
once around the Sun.

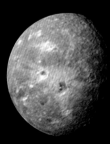

« Uranus has 27 moons.
Most of them are made
of ice and rock.

●— **Uranus**

Puck

●

Miranda

Ariel

Umbriel

Titania

Oberon

Miranda

⌃ **Uranus's moon Miranda is covered with craters, grooves, and cliffs.**

Uranus is a gas giant four times bigger than Earth. It is so far away and faint that it was only discovered in 1781.

Neptune

Neptune is the farthest planet from the Sun. It takes Neptune 165 years to travel around the Sun.

⌄ **Streaky white clouds appear bright against the planet's blue color.**

>> **The huge, dark area is a storm in Neptune's atmosphere.**

⌃ **Neptune's biggest moon, Triton, is covered with ice volcanoes.**

Neptune is a gas giant nearly four times the size of the Earth. It has the strongest winds in the Solar System. Sometimes dark storms or clouds appear on Neptune.

Dwarf planets

The dwarf planets are smaller than the main planets. Most of them are made of ice.

>> Pluto was once called a planet, but it was renamed a dwarf planet in 2006.

Eris

Haumea

Makemake

Ceres

<< Four of the dwarf planets are shown here.

Ceres is found between Mars and Jupiter. All the other dwarf planets are found far beyond Neptune, in a zone called the Kuiper Belt.

˅ **The Kuiper Belt is made up of millions of icy and rocky objects that orbit the Sun.**

Comets

Comets are city-sized chunks of ice and dirt. They move around the Sun following egg-shaped paths.

⌄ **Most comets come from the Oort Cloud. This is a zone halfway between the Sun and our next nearest star.**

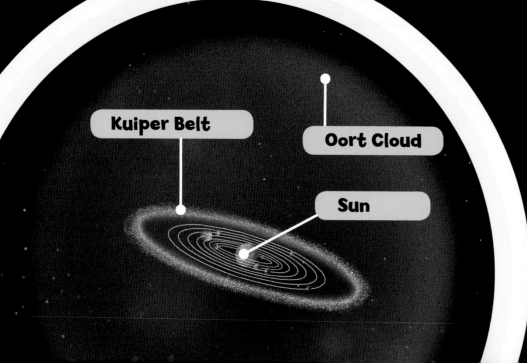

Kuiper Belt

Oort Cloud

Sun

⌃ **Halley's Comet, named after astronomer Edmond Halley, appears every 76 years.**

As comets approach the Sun, they start to melt and give off gas and dust. Glowing in the sunlight, the gas and dust make long, bright tails.

« At the center of a comet is a huge, icy ball of dirt.

Earth

Asteroids

Asteroids are lumps of
rock that orbit the Sun.
Sometimes they hit
planets and make craters.

⌃ Eros is an
asteroid about
the size of a city.

« An asteroid hit
Earth 65 million
years ago and wiped
out the dinosaurs.

>> **Small asteroids break up in Earth's atmosphere.**

There are thousands of asteroids in the Asteroid Belt, between Mars and Jupiter. The biggest are the size of a small country. Others are smaller than a football field.

Meteorites

Meteorites are lumps of rock or iron that have fallen to Earth.

>> Shooting stars, or meteors, are bright trails of light in the night sky.

<< The world's biggest meteorite lies where it fell, in Namibia, Africa. It weighs nearly 60 tons.

☆ **Lumps of rock land on other planets, too. This one was found on Mars.**

As the lumps of rock fall to Earth, they heat up in the atmosphere. They can be seen as bright meteors or "shooting stars" that fly across the sky.

Stars

A star is a large ball of hot, burning gas. Stars shine by burning gas to make heat and light.

⌄ **Many stars are found in groups, called clusters.**

Our Sun is the nearest star to the Earth. Other stars are so far away that they look like tiny dots of light and can only be seen at night.

« Our Sun is a medium-sized yellow star.

⌃ Stars come in different colors and sizes.

Life of a star

Like people, stars are born, grow old, and die. Stars can live for billions of years.

>> Blue giants are large, hot stars that live short lives.

Blue giant

Yellow dwarf (the Sun)

>> Red dwarves are cooler stars that burn more slowly and live longer.

Stars are born inside huge clouds of dust and gas. As they grow older they get bigger.

Most stars fade and cool when they run out of gas. But the biggest stars explode in a **supernova**.

∧ This cloud of gas and dust is full of newborn stars.

37

Constellations

Constellations are groups of stars that make patterns in the sky.

Southern Hemisphere

Northern Hemisphere

⌃ **Different constellations can be seen in the Northern and Southern Hemispheres.**

>> Orion can be seen here shining brightly in the night sky.

There are 88 constellations in the sky. Most of them are named after characters, creatures, and objects from ancient legends.

>> Orion was named after a hunter. Three bright stars make his belt.

Galaxies

A galaxy is a massive group of stars, gas, and dust moving through space.

⌄ **Most galaxies are so far away that they can only be seen through a telescope.**

⌄ **Sometimes galaxies crash into each other as they move through space.**

There are hundreds of billions of galaxies in the universe. They come in many shapes and sizes. Some belong to big groups of galaxies called clusters.

« Spiral galaxies look like whirlpools.

The Milky Way

The Milky Way is the galaxy we live in. It is a flattened spiral shape.

⌄ **The Sun is located on one of the Milky Way's spiral arms.**

⌃ From Earth, you
can sometimes see
a small part of the
Milky Way.

⌃ The Milky
Way is made up
of hundreds of
billions of stars.

Most of the stars in the
Milky Way are so faint that
they blend into a misty
band. On a clear night,
we can see this band
stretching across the sky.

The universe

The universe contains everything you can think of, from your home to the farthest, faintest galaxies in space!

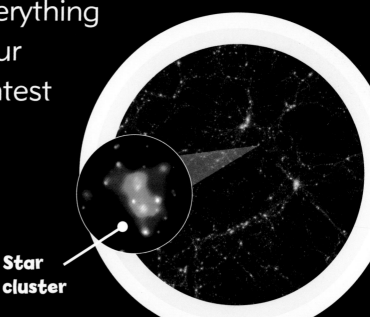

Star cluster

⌃ Clusters of galaxies make a spiderweb pattern in space.

⌃ This photo shows the faintest and most distant galaxies ever seen.

Astronomers think there are probably about 1,000 billion galaxies in the universe. But no one knows how far it stretches, or what lies beyond it.

« Gas, dust, and planets make up the parts of the universe that we can see.

Stargazing

To look at the stars, find a dark place away from bright city lights.

You can see some amazing sights from your backyard, such as the Orion Nebula.

Looking through binoculars will help you see star colors more easily. Binoculars can also reveal details on the Moon's surface.

« Binoculars aren't as powerful as telescopes, but are much less expensive.

⌄ Through binoculars, you can see craters on the Moon.

Crater

Telescopes

Telescopes make distant objects appear closer. Astronomers use them to study space.

<< **Refracting telescopes use** lenses **to make an image appear larger.**

>> Radio telescopes collect radio waves from far out in space and use them to create images.

⌄ The Hubble Space Telescope is in orbit around Earth.

Some telescopes use lenses and mirrors to collect light and make an image. Others can see energy that is invisible to the eye, such as **radio waves** and **x-rays**.

Rockets

Rockets are used to launch spacecraft from Earth's surface, through the atmosphere and into space.

« The first rocket to reach space was the German V-2 rocket in 1942.

<< **The moment a rocket leaves the ground is called "blast-off."**

^ **Rockets are the only type of engine that can work in space.**

Rockets fly when very hot gases are blasted from a hole at their base. The rocket moves upward, away from the gases.

Satellites

Satellites orbit planets or stars. Some are natural, such as moons. Others are machines launched to orbit Earth.

˅ **Thousands of man-made satellites orbit Earth.**

˄ **Russia's Sputnik 1 was the first satellite, launched in 1957.**

Some satellites beam television signals and cell phone calls around the world. Others help us to find out exactly where we are on the planet.

ᵛ **Some satellites are powered by** solar panels.

Solar panel

Astronauts

People who have been into space are called astronauts. Only a few hundred people have ever been in space.

∧ **Yuri Gagarin, the first astronaut, went to space in 1961.**

>> **Astronauts must do lots of training before they go into space.**

HST
JSC WETF 131

<< **Astronauts wear protective space suits to leave their spacecraft.**

In space there is no **gravity**—the force that keeps you on the ground—so everything floats around. This makes simple tasks like washing your hair very difficult.

The first men on the Moon

On July 20, 1969, a spacecraft with three people on board touched down on the Moon for the first time.

>> Buzz Aldrin (shown here) and Neil Armstrong were the first men to walk on the Moon.

« **The Saturn V (Saturn Five) rocket launched the Apollo missions to the Moon.**

The landing was part of the United States's Apollo program. A further five Apollo missions landed on the Moon.

˅ **An electric moon buggy was used on the final three Apollo missions.**

International Space Station

The International Space Station (ISS) is a science lab and **observatory** in orbit around Earth.

⌃ **The bright streak seen here above the Moon shows the path taken by the ISS.**

Picture credits